One Day One Night

CYCLES IN NATURE

DAVID DREW

Illustrated by Robert Roennfeldt

RIGBY

About this book

Suppose there were two islands on opposite sides of the Earth: Up-Over and Down-Under.

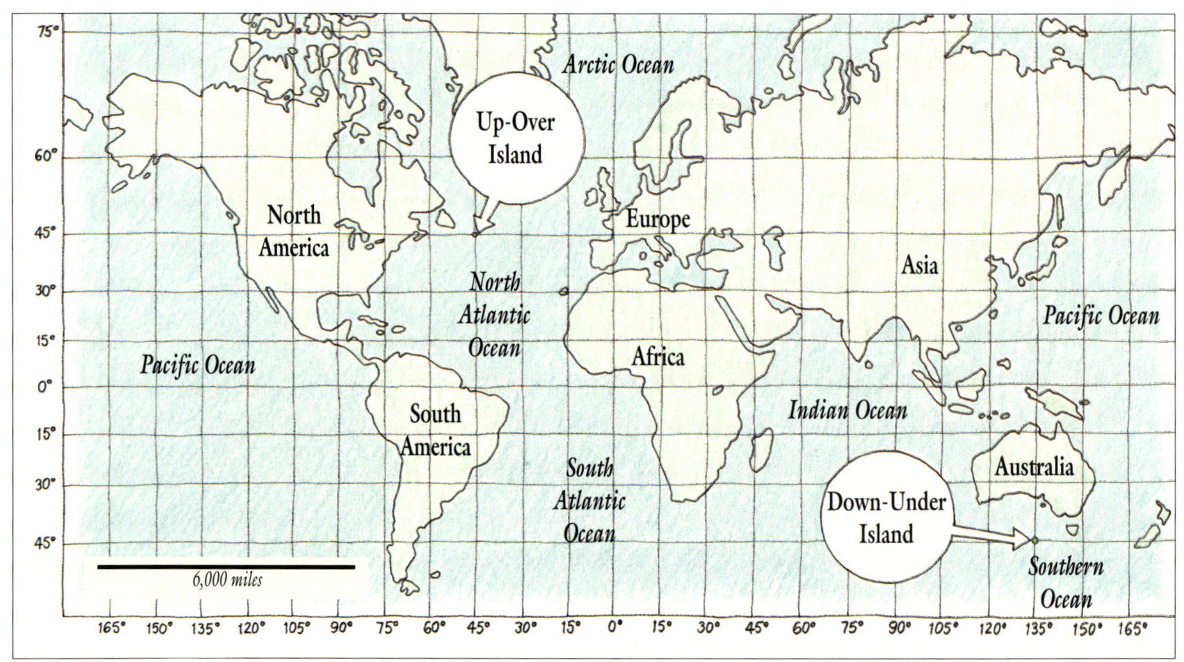

• When it is midday on Up-Over, it is midnight on Down-Under.

• When it is autumn on Up-Over, it is spring on Down-Under.

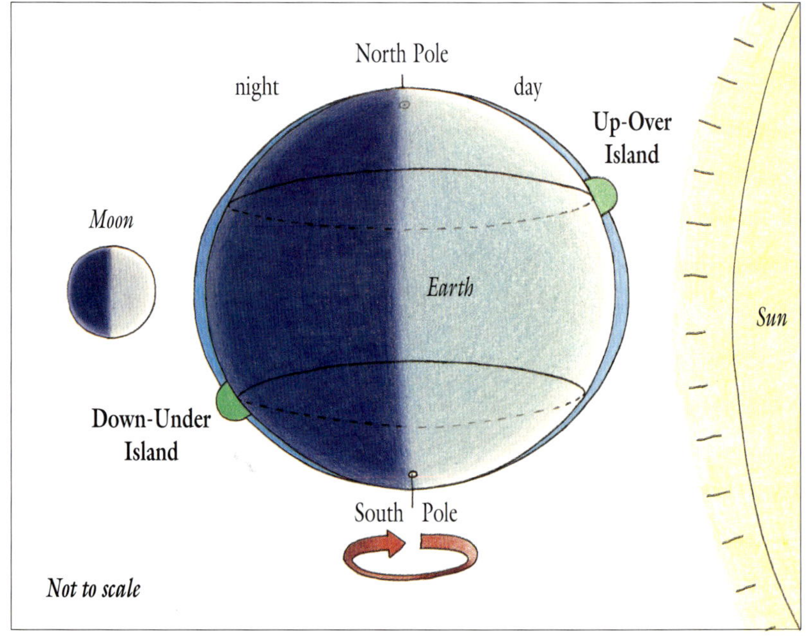

2

Read the pictures

The pictures in this book show what happens in a day and a night on the islands of Up-Over and Down-Under.

All the information is in the pictures:

- **Find and tell** what happens. You can tell it as a story, time line, map, diary, graph, table, or storyboard.
- **Check back** to see what has changed in each picture, and why.
- **Figure out** the connections, for example, between the weather and the barometer, or between the Sun, the Moon, and the tides.
- **Predict** what might happen before turning each page.

There are many stories to find and tell. *Look for these characters:* Sonny Daley, his mom, and grandpa

Star Knightley, her dad, and grandma

and look for these: a raccoon, a bathtub, a sunflower, a scarf, a sailing ship,

and an umbrella.

There are many other things to find and talk about, as well.

6 a.m. on Up-Over Island

- **Find and tell** the story of the dog.
- **Check back:** where is the Daley family and what are they doing?
- **Figure out:** are you facing north or south? What season is it?
- **Predict:** where will the Sun be in three hours?

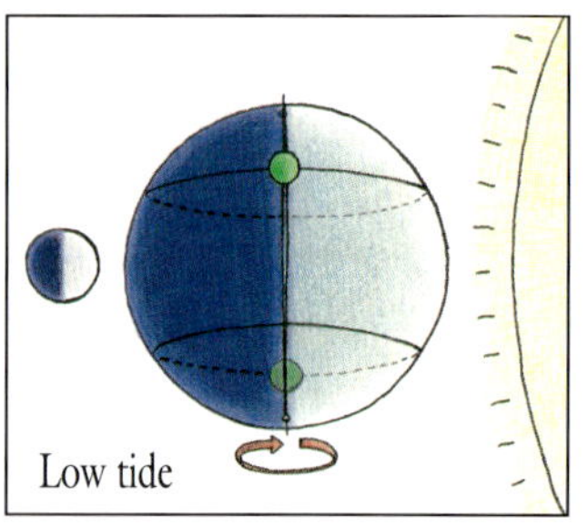

6 p.m. on Down-Under Island

- **Find and tell** the story of the possum.
- **Check back:** where is Star's family and what are they doing?
- **Figure out:** are you facing north or south?
- **Predict:** where will the Moon be in three hours? Will the tide rise or fall?

Sunrise

You can also make up your own questions. Ask a friend to answer them.

Sunset

What will change in 3 hours' time?

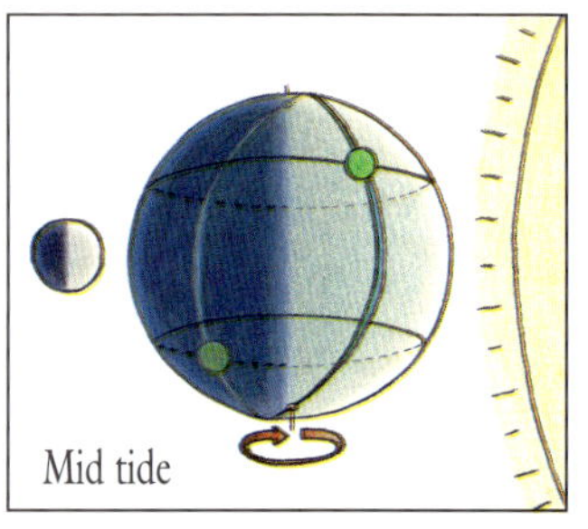

Mid tide

Morning

What has changed?

Evening

What will change in 3 hours' time?

12 *midday* on Up-Over Island

• **Find and tell** the story of the crab and the seagulls.
• **Check back:** has the temperature changed?
• **Figure out:** how does the barometer change when it rains?
• **Predict:** who will rescue the cow?

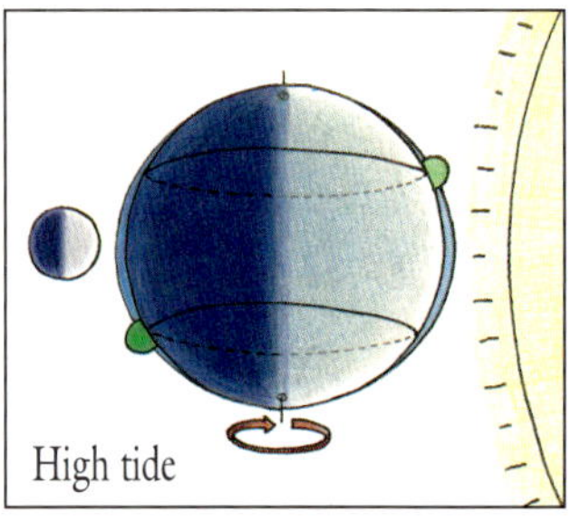

High tide

12 *midnight* on Down-Under Island

• **Find and tell** the story of the white cat.
• **Check back:** what do moonflowers do at night? *(Look for them below the clock tower.)*
• **Figure out:** are all three clocks telling the same time?
• **Predict:** what will happen to Aquila?

Midday

What has changed?

Midnight

What will change in 3 hours' time?

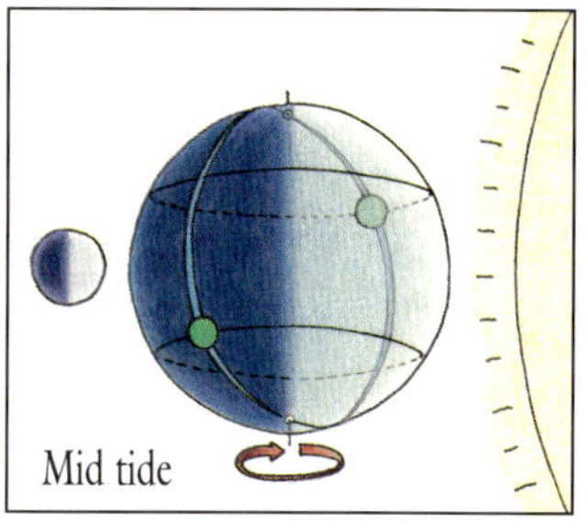

Afternoon

What has changed?

Early hours

What will change in 3 hours' time?

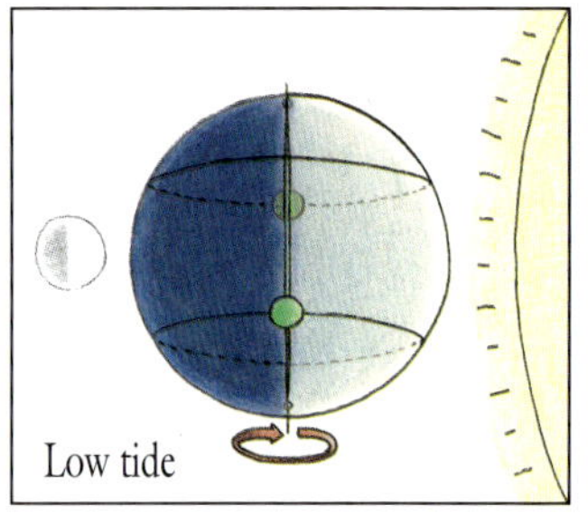

6 p.m. on Up-Over Island

- **Find and tell** the story of the cow.
- **Check back:** what has grandpa been doing?
- **Figure out** what happens to the temperature at night.
- **Predict:** what will the spider do next?

6 a.m. on Down-Under Island

- **Find and tell** the story of the caterpillar.
- **Check back:** how has the windmill changed, and why?
- **Figure out:** what is the effect of the Sun on the sunflower?
- **Predict:** Look at the barometer. What will happen next?

Sunset

What has changed?

Sunrise

What will change in 3 hours' time?

9 p.m. on Up-Over Island

- **Find and tell** the story of the raccoon.
- **Check back:** what did grandpa take to the beach?
- **Figure out:** what happens to daisy flowers at night?
- **Predict:** where will the full Moon be at midnight?

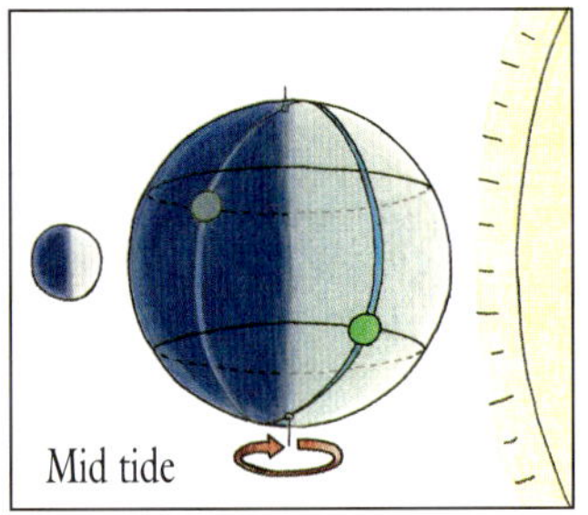

Mid tide

9 a.m. on Down-Under Island

- **Find and tell** the story of the nestlings.
- **Check back:** find the nocturnal animals and the diurnal animals.
- **Figure out:** what has Star made with the stick and the stones?
- **Predict:** what is the lamb about to do?

What has changed?

What will change in 3 hours' time?

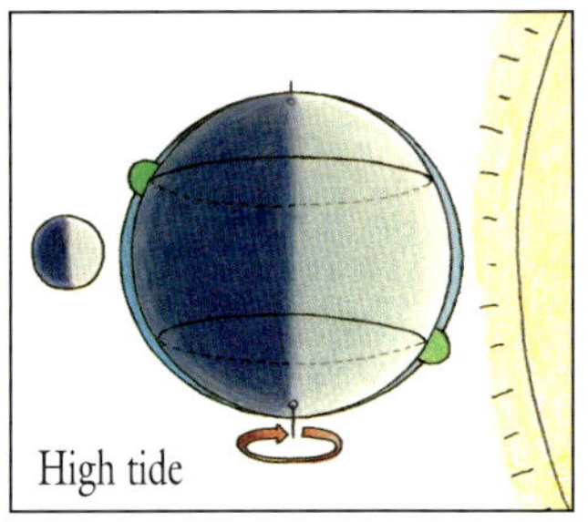

12 *midnight* on Up-Over Island

- **Find and tell** the story of the spider.
- **Check back and figure out:** are the Down-Under stars (pages 6–11) the same as these stars, or different?
- **Predict:** what constellation will appear at 3 a.m.?

12 *midday* on Down-Under Island

- **Find and tell** the story of the ewe and the lamb.
- **Check back:** what is happening in the water trough?
- **Figure out** how Star's sundial works.
- **Predict:** what will happen to the kite after the storm passes?

What has changed?

What will change in 3 hours' time?

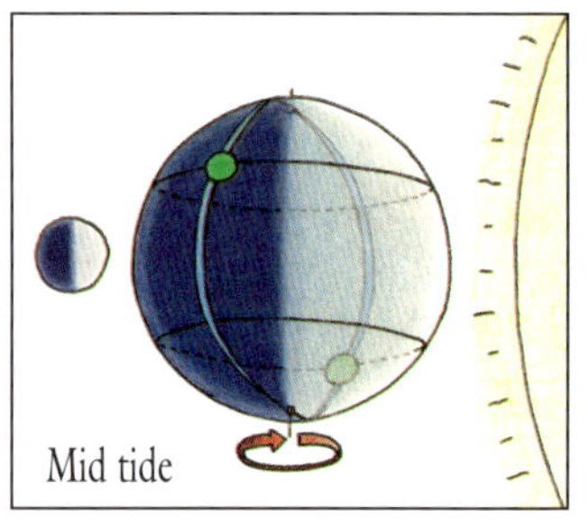

What has changed?

What will change in 3 hours' time?

6 a.m. on Up-Over Island

- **Find and tell** how both the islands have changed in 24 hours.
- **Check back:** where would the stars be if we could see them?
- **Figure out:** why is the sunrise almost one minute later today?
- **Predict:** what season will it be in 3 months?

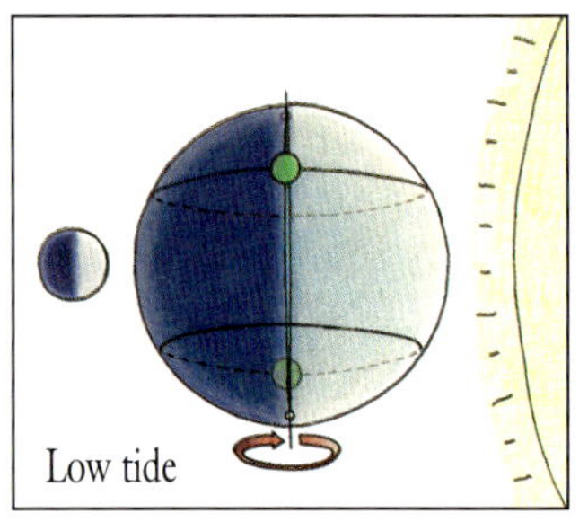

6 p.m. on Down-Under Island

- **Tell** tomorrow's story on each island.
- **Check back:** what are the Knightleys having for dinner?
- **Figure out:** where does the water in the trough come from?
- **Predict:** what will the weather be like in 3 months?

Sunrise

What has changed?

Sunset

Now, what will change in 3 **months**' time?

6 a.m. on Up-Over Island, *December 22nd*

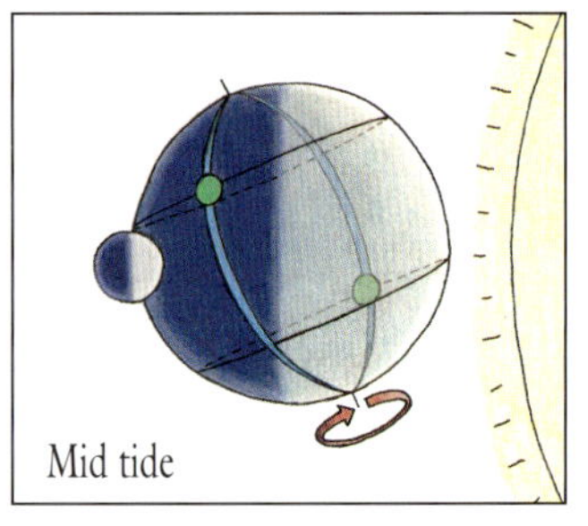

- **Check back:** where did mom's scarf come from?
- **Figure out:** why is the sky still dark?
- **Predict:** draw both islands as they will be in 3 months' time.

6 p.m. on Down-Under Island, *December 22nd*

- **Check back:** what happened to the lamb and the caterpillar?
- **Figure out** how far the sailing ship has travelled in 3 months.
- **Predict:** draw both islands as they will be in 3 months' time.

Before dawn

What has changed?

Late afternoon

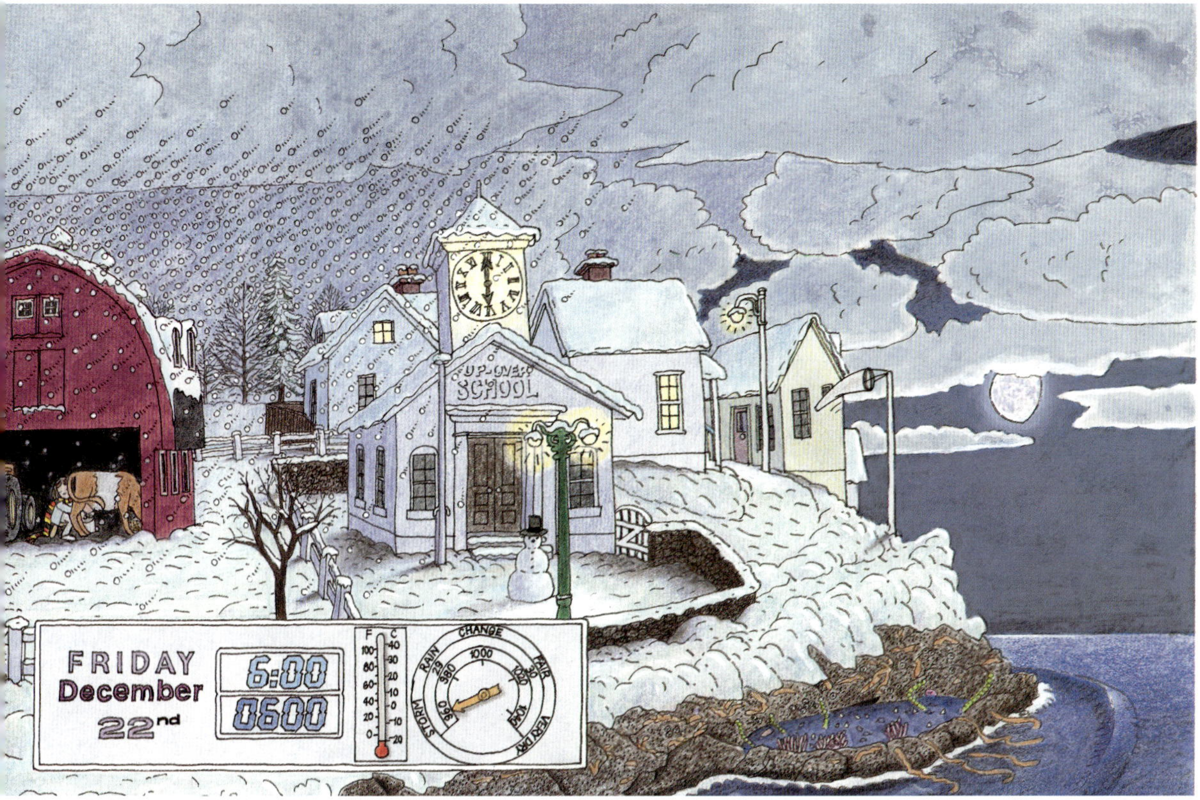

UP-OVER SCHOOL

FRIDAY
December
22nd

6:00
0600

RAIN   CHANGE   FAIR
STORMY   VERY DRY

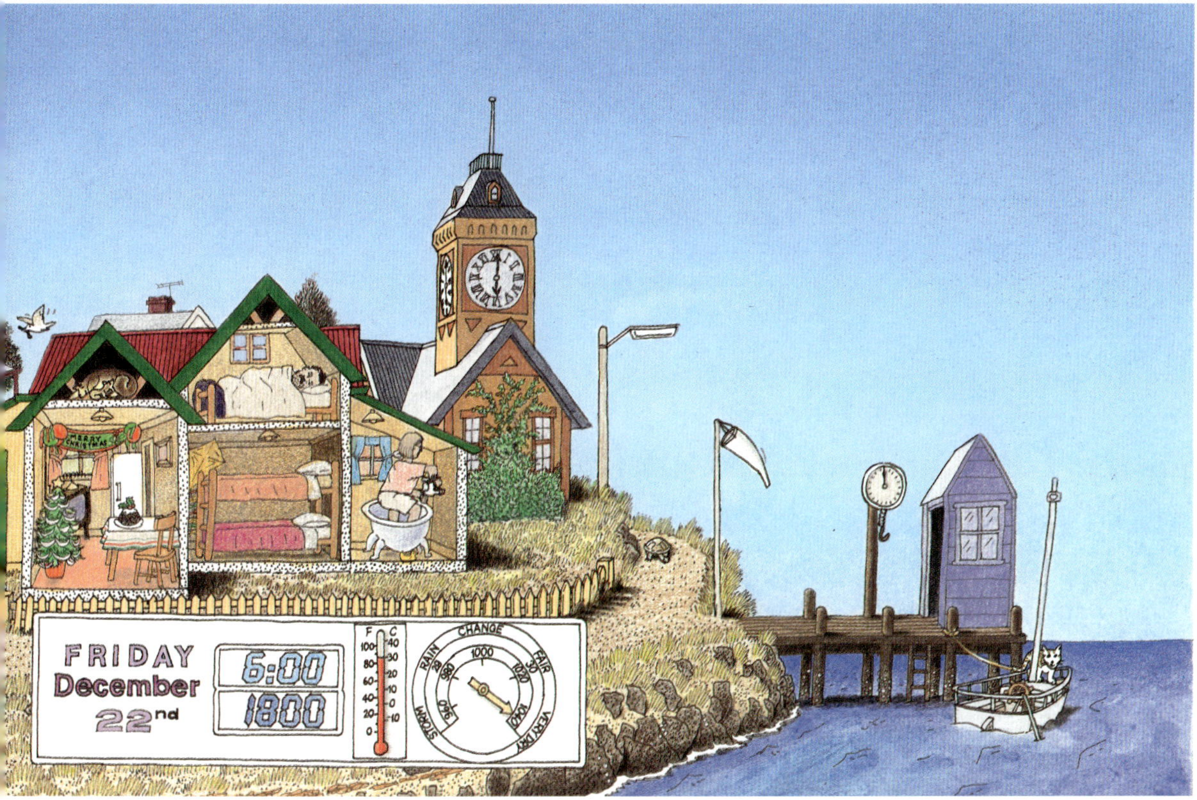

FRIDAY
December
22nd

6:00
1800

MERRY CHRISTMAS

EAST WEST